Popular Music Theory

Theory

Grade Four

---

by

Camilla Sheldon & Tony Skinner

5909329161

A CIP record for this publication is available from the British Library.

ISBN: 1-898466-44-0

First edition © 2001 Registry Publications Ltd.

Published in Great Britain by

Registry House, Churchill Mews, Dennett Rd, Croydon, Surrey, CR0 3JH

Typesetting by

Take Note Publishing Limited, Lingfield, Surrey

Original drawings of pop performers by Chris Challinor.
Instrument photographs supplied by John Hornby Skewes Ltd.
Printed in Great Britain by MFP, Manchester.

———— Contents ————

Introduction

This book covers all the new material you need to know to take the London College of Music Grade Four examination in Popular Music Theory.

As well as helping you to pass the examination, the intention of this book is to introduce and explain the theory behind popular music and so help you improve your musicianship. You can benefit from working through the book whether or not you intend to take an examination. You will benefit most if you try out the information you learn in this book in a practical music-making setting, by relating the information to your instrument and by using it to create your own music.

This book is part of a series that offers a structured and progressive approach to understanding the theory of popular music and whilst it can be used for independent study, it is ideally intended as a supplement to group or individual tuition.

The chapters of the book follow the sections of the examination. Each chapter outlines the facts you need to know for the examination, together with the theory behind the facts. Each chapter is completed with some examples of the types of questions that will appear in the examination paper. The sample questions are intended to provide a clear guide as to the kind of questions that may be asked in the examination, however the list of questions is neither exclusive nor exhaustive. Once you've worked through the questions at the end of each section, you can check your answers by looking at the 'sample answers' in the back of the book.

As the requirements for each examination are cumulative, it is essential that you have a knowledge of the requirements for the previous grades. If you are not already familiar with this earlier material, it is recommended that you study the preceding handbooks in this series.

Examinations are held twice a year and you can only enter for an examination by completing the stamped entry form at the back of each handbook.

We hope you enjoy working through this book and wish you success with the examination and all your musical endeavours.

Camilla Sheldon and Tony Skinner

In the examination, you can use either the treble clef (G clef) or the bass clef (F clef) to write your answers. The basics of reading and writing music notation are covered in the earlier books in this series. Below are a few 'reminder notes'.

key signatures

Key signatures are written at the start of every staff of music. Each particular key signature is always written in the same way, with the flats and sharps being placed in a progressive order on specific lines and spaces (as shown below).

accidentals

When a flat, sharp or natural sign is written before a note during a piece of music it is called an *accidental*.

A *natural* (♮) sign means that the note is returned to its 'natural' version. For example: C♯ would become C, E♭ would become E.

musical terms

Sometimes there are two different names that can be used for the same musical element. Also, the terminology that is widely used in N. America (and increasingly amongst pop, rock and jazz musicians in the U.K. and elsewhere) is different to that traditionally used in the U.K. and other parts of Europe.

A summary of the main alternative terms is shown below. In the examination you can use either version. In this book we generally use the terms shown in the left-hand column, as these are the ones that are more commonly used amongst popular music musicians.

whole note	=	semibreve
half note	=	minim
quarter note	=	crotchet
eighth note	=	quaver
sixteenth note	=	semiquaver
whole step	=	whole tone
half step	=	semitone
staff	=	stave
treble clef	=	G clef
bass clef	=	F clef
measures	=	bars
keynote	=	tonic
$\frac{4}{4}$	=	𝄴
flag	=	tail
leger line	=	ledger line
flattened 3rd, 6th or 7th	=	minor 3rd, 6th or 7th
flattened 5th	=	diminished 5th

Section One – scales and keys

In this section of the exam you may be asked to write out and identify any of the following scales (and their key signatures):

Scales with key signatures to the range of three sharps and three flats:

- major
- natural minor
- harmonic minor
- Blues scales: C, G, D, A, F, B♭ and E♭

- pentatonic major
- pentatonic minor

The scales that have been added for the Grade Four exam are:

- major: A and E♭
- natural minor: F# and C
- harmonic minor: A, E, B, F#, D, G and C
- blues: A and E♭

- pentatonic major: A and E♭
- pentatonic minor: F# and C

In this book we will only cover in detail these additional scales, so if you are unsure about any of the other requirements you should study the previous handbooks in this series.

So that the scales learnt in theory can be used effectively in a practical way, you should be able to do the following:

- Write out, and identify, the *letter names* that make up each scale.

- Write out, and identify, each scale in standard *music notation* (adding or identifying the key signature where appropriate). You can write your answers in either the treble clef or the bass clef.

- Write out, or identify, the *scale spelling* of each scale.

the theory

major & natural minor scales

Major scales are constructed using the pattern of whole steps and half steps shown below:

W W H W W W H

Here is the E♭ major scale as an example.

notes: E♭   F   G   A♭   B♭   C   D   E♭
pattern: W   W   H   W   W   W   H

Notice that, apart from the repetition of the keynote at the octave, *each letter name is used only once*. This rule applies to all scales at this grade (apart from the fifth degree of the blues scale) and ensures that the correct *enharmonic spelling* is used for each scale. For example, in the E♭ major scale shown above, notice how a half step above G becomes A♭, rather than G#.

Natural minor scales are constructed using the following step-pattern. (Notice that it is the same step-pattern as if the major scale pattern had started on its sixth degree).

W H W W H W W

For example, here is the F# natural minor scale.

notes: **F♯ G♯ A B C♯ D E F♯**
pattern: **W H W W H W W**

A natural minor:	A B C D E F G A
A harmonic minor:	A B C D E F G♯ A
F♯ natural minor:	F♯ G♯ A B C♯ D E F♯
F♯ harmonic minor:	F♯ G♯ A B C♯ D E♯ F♯
C natural minor:	C D E♭ F G A♭ B♭ C
C harmonic minor:	C D E♭ F G A♭ B C

pentatonic scales

Pentatonic major scales are made up of five notes taken from the major scale with the same keynote. The five notes are the 1st, 2nd, 3rd, 5th and 6th. Notice that it is the 4th and 7th notes of the major scale that are omitted to create a pentatonic major scale. The notes in the E♭ pentatonic major scale are therefore E♭, F, G, B♭ and C. (When played or written as a scale the octave is also included.)

Pentatonic minor scales are made up of five notes (the 1st, 3rd, 4th, 5th and 7th) taken from the natural minor scale with the same keynote. Notice that it is the 2nd and 6th notes of the natural minor scale that are omitted to create a pentatonic minor scale. The notes in the F# pentatonic minor scale are therefore F#, A, B, C# and E. (When played or written as a scale the octave is also included.)

harmonic minor scales

The harmonic minor scale contains the same notes as the natural minor scale (starting on the same keynote) *except that*, in the harmonic minor scale, the note on the seventh degree is raised a half step. This gives the harmonic minor scale a very distinctive sound, because it has a large interval (of three half steps) between its sixth and seventh degrees.

The following table shows some examples contrasting the difference between natural minor and harmonic minor scales.

blues scales

The *blues scale* is a six-note scale. It uses notes from the major scale, but lowers some of them. The notes taken from the major scale are the 1st, 3rd, 4th, 5th and 7th, however the 3rd, 5th and 7th notes are all lowered by one half step (semitone) to create the *blue notes*. The ♭3rd and ♭7th notes replace the 3rd and 7th notes of the major scale, but the ♭5th note is used *in addition to* the 5th note of the major scale. The blues scale therefore contains the 1st, ♭3rd, 4th, ♭5th, 5th and ♭7th. For example, the notes in the C blues scale are C, E♭, F, G♭, G and B♭. (When played or written as a scale the octave is also included.)

♭5 / #4

The ♭5 note within the blues scale is sometimes referred to as a #4. For example, in the C blues scale, G♭ may be called F# by some musicians. This is because in music notation it is traditionally 'correct' to avoid writing two notes on the 5th degree of the scale, hence the #4 note is used instead. However, blues does not readily conform to the traditions of standard music notation and the term ♭5 is now commonly used (and notated) in the blues scale amongst blues, jazz and rock musicians. For this reason, whenever referring to the blues scale in this book, the term ♭5 will be used and the notes and scale numbers will be named accordingly.

In the exam, you can use either term – ♭5 or #4 – with the appropriate note names and scale numbers, but you must be consistent in your use.

---

scale notes

Here are examples of all the scale types that are required for the Grade Four exam.

A major:		A	B	C#	D	E	F#	G#	A
Eb major:		Eb	F	G	Ab	Bb	C	D	Eb
A pentatonic major:			A	B	C#	E	F#	A
Eb pentatonic major:			Eb	F	G	Bb	C	Eb

F# natural minor:	F#	G#	A	B	C#	D	E	F#
C natural minor:	C	D	Eb	F	G	Ab	Bb	C
F# pentatonic minor:		F#	A	B	C#	E	F#
C pentatonic minor:		C	Eb	F	G	Bb	C

A blues:		A	C	D	Eb	E	G	A
Eb blues:		Eb	Gb	Ab	Bbb	Bb	Db	Eb

A harmonic minor:	A	B	C	D	E	F	G#	A
C harmonic minor:	C	D	Eb	F	G	Ab	B	C
F# harmonic minor:	F#	G#	A	B	C#	D	E#	F#

You should try and play these scales on your instrument so that you can hear the sound of them. It will also help you to memorise the notes that make up each scale. If you forget the names of the notes in these scales, you can work them out in the following way:

For major and natural minor scales: use the 'step-pattern' to work out the notes of the scale.

For pentatonic major and minor scales: use the procedure described above to work out the appropriate major or natural minor scale and then select the five notes that you need for the pentatonic scale you require.

For harmonic minor scales: work out the appropriate natural minor scale using the 'step-pattern' and then raise the 7th note of the scale by a half step.

For blues scales: work out the appropriate major scale using the 'step-pattern', and then select the six notes you need for the blues scale, lowering the appropriate notes by a half step. Remember that you need to include the b5th and the ♮ 5th notes.

Remember that for every scale (apart from the on fifth degree of the blues scale) each letter name should be used only once (apart from the repetition of the keynote at the octave).

key signatures and scale notation

Every key signature represents both a major and its relative minor key.

For example:

Three sharps – F#, C# and G# – is the key signature for both A major and F# minor.

Three flats – Bb, Eb and Ab – is the key signature for both Eb major and C minor.

You can usually identify whether the key of a piece of music is major or minor by its overall sound; sometimes you can also identify this by seeing which note the melody begins or ends with. If a piece of music has three flats in the key signature and begins and ends on an Eb note it is likely to be in the key of Eb major; if it begins and ends on a C note it is likely to be in C minor. If the chords are shown, then you can normally identify the key from the first and last chord.

In music notation key signatures are written, after the clef, at the start of the music and are repeated on every staff.

The key signatures and scale notation for the major, pentatonic major, natural minor and pentatonic minor scales which have been added for the Grade Four exam, are shown opposite.

A major

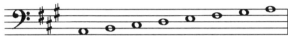

Eb major

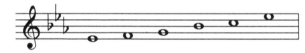

A pentatonic major

Eb pentatonic major

F# natural minor

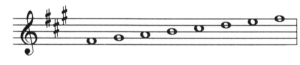

C natural minor

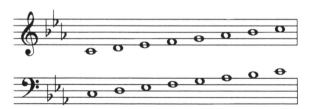

F# pentatonic minor

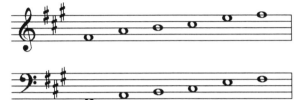

C pentatonic minor

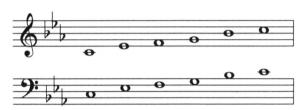

writing harmonic minor scales

Harmonic minor scales are written using the appropriate minor key signature and then using an accidental to raise the note on the seventh degree of the scale by a half step.

- If the seventh note is a natural, according to the key signature, then the accidental will need to be a sharp. For example, the key signature for F# minor means that the 7th degree is E natural, so in the scale of F# harmonic minor the 7th note will be E#.

- If the 7th note is a flat, according to the key signature, then the accidental will be a natural. For example, the key signature for C minor means that the 7th degree is Bb, so in the scale of C harmonic minor the 7th note will be B♮.

Here are some examples of the harmonic minor scales which areset for the Grade Four exam.

A harmonic minor

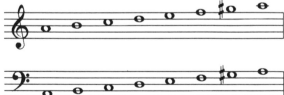

F# harmonic minor

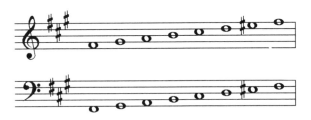

C harmonic minor

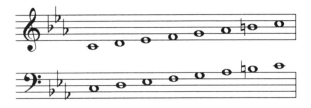

blues key signatures

Blues music does not fit neatly into the traditional rules of music theory that were originally developed for classical music. Because blues scales have a minor third interval between the 1st and 3rd notes of the scale, it might appear that they should use minor key signatures. However, it is generally considered that major key signatures are more appropriate for blues. The reason for this is that blues music is normally based on 'dominant harmony' – in other words, the chordal accompaniment to a blues usually consists of dominant 7th chords. As dominant 7th chords are essentially 'major' chords, this creates an underlying 'major harmony' which is best reflected by the use of major key signatures. The fact that the melody or improvisation uses *flattened* notes against these major chords is simply a reflection of the method that blues music uses to create the musical tensions that form the core of the 'blues' sound.

Although using major key signatures means that a number of accidentals will have to be used when notating music taken from the blues scale, this is actually an advantage as it immediately demonstrates to the reader that the written music is blues-based and not in a standard major or minor key.

The key signature for each blues scale is therefore the same as for the major scale with the same starting pitch. For example, the A blues scale has a key signature of three sharps – F#, C# and G# and the Eb blues scale has a key signature of three flats – Bb, Eb and Ab.

Remember that the above is a combination of two musical traditions and reflects the most common current usage. For blues scales and keys, the key signature only tells you what the key centre is – it does NOT tell you which notes are in the scale. In fact, each blues scale will need to use several accidentals as a result of the key signature.

A blues

Eb blues

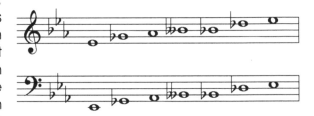

Enharmonic spellings

The Bbb note in the Eb blues scale is another way of describing the pitch of 'A'; just as the Cb in the F blues scale is the same pitch as 'B'. Whilst there would be no difference in the sound of either version, it is important in all scales that the pitch name of the note matches its interval number. The Eb blues scale uses a 'double flat' to notate the b5th because it is the fifth note (Bb) which is lowered and not the fourth note (Ab) which is raised.

---

scale spellings

In popular music, instead of using the letter names of the notes in a scale, musicians often use numbers. This is called the *scale spelling*. Each note of the scale is given a number, starting with the keynote as '1'. For example, in E♭ major the notes would be numbered as follows:

$$E\flat \quad F \quad G \quad A\flat \quad B\flat \quad C \quad D \quad E\flat$$
$$1 \quad 2 \quad 3 \quad 4 \quad 5 \quad 6 \quad 7 \quad 8$$

The numbers refer to the *intervals* between the keynote and each other note in the scale. For example, rather than talking about the B♭ note in the scale of E♭, pop musicians might refer to it as the 5th in the key of E♭.

Each type of scale has a unique scale spelling. This enables easy comparison between different scale types.

Major scales are numbered like this:

> 1 2 3 4 5 6 7 8

All other scales are numbered in comparison to the major scale.

Natural minor scales are numbered like this:

> 1 2 ♭3 4 5 ♭6 ♭7 8

Harmonic minor scales are numbered like this:

> 1 2 ♭3 4 5 ♭6 7 8

There follows a brief explanation as to why the natural minor and harmonic minor scales are numbered this way. In the exam, however, you will only be asked to identify, or write out the scale spellings.

Supplementary explanation

The appearance of a ♭ sign in a scale spelling does not mean that the note which occurs on that scale degree is necessarily a flat note. Instead, the flat sign is used, in this instance, as a method of indicating that this scale degree creates a 'minor' (i.e. smaller) interval when compared to the major scale - i.e. the distance between the keynote and this scale degree is a half step smaller than the distance between the keynote and the corresponding scale degree in the major scale with the same starting note. For example, the interval between G and B♭ (the third degree of the G natural minor scale) is a half step smaller than the interval between G and B (the third degree of the G major scale). In fact, the 3rd and 6th degrees of the natural minor and harmonic minor scales, and the 7th degree of the natural minor scale, are all minor intervals when compared to the major scale. (You can work this out for yourself by counting the number of half steps between the keynotes and these degrees of the scales). Although the meaning is exactly the same, pop musicians generally prefer to call these intervals 'flattened' (rather than minor), and consequently a ♭ is placed before them to indicate this.

Pentatonic major scales are numbered like this:

> 1 2 3 5 6 8

The scale spelling of the pentatonic major scale is based on that of the major scale, but because the pentatonic major scale doesn't include the 4th or 7th notes of the major scale, these scale numbers are omitted.

Pentatonic minor scales are numbered like this:

`1 ♭3 4 5 ♭7 8`

The scale spelling of the pentatonic minor scale is based on the natural minor scale, but because the pentatonic minor scale doesn't include the 2nd or ♭6th notes of the natural minor scale, these scale numbers are omitted.

Blues scales are numbered like this:

`1 ♭3 4 ♭5 5 ♭7 8`

Below you will find a brief explanation as to why the blues scale is numbered this way. In the exam, however, you will only be asked to identify, or write out the scale spelling.

Supplementary explanation

The scale spelling of the blues scale is numbered in comparison to the major scale. The blues scale contains the 4th and 5th notes of the major scale, but not the 2nd or 6th notes. The 3rd and 7th notes are *flattened* in comparison to the major scale, as the intervals between the keynote and these scale degrees are a half step smaller than the intervals between the keynote and the same scale degrees in the major scale.

The additional note – the ♭5th – is called a *flattened* (or *diminished*) interval. This is because it is one half step smaller than the 5th note which is also contained in the scale. The full name for the interval between the 1st and 5th notes in all the scales covered so far (including the blues scale) is a *perfect fifth*. Unlike the other intervals we have looked at, when *perfect 5th* intervals are made smaller by one half step they are not called 'minor' 5th intervals, instead they are known as *flattened* (or *diminished*) 5th intervals.

---

comparing scales

You can use your knowledge of major scales and scale spellings to work out the notes contained in all other scales. For example, by knowing which notes are contained in the G major scale it is possible to work out which notes are contained in the other scale types.

major scale:	1	2	3	4	5	6	7	8
G major:	G	A	B	C	D	E	F#	G
pentatonic major:	1	2	3		5	6		8
G pentatonic major:	G	A	B		D	E		G
natural minor:	1	2	♭3	4	5	♭6	♭7	8
G natural minor:	G	A	B♭	C	D	E♭	F	G
harmonic minor:	1	2	♭3	4	5	♭6	7	8
G harmonic minor:	G	A	B♭	C	D	E♭	F♯	G
pentatonic minor:	1	♭3	4	5	♭7	8		
G pentatonic minor:	G	B♭	C	D	F	G		
blues:	1	♭3	4	♭5	5	♭7	8	
G blues:	G	B♭	C	D♭	D	F	G	

Alternatively, scales can also be compared directly with each other (without reference to the major scale). For example:

■ the pentatonic minor scale is the same as the natural minor scale but with the 2nd and 6th notes omitted.

■ the harmonic minor scale is the same as the natural minor scale but with the 7th note raised by a half step.

■ the blues scale, except for the addition of the ♭5th note, is exactly the same as the pentatonic minor scale.

the exam

Below are some examples of the types of questions that candidates may be asked in this section of the exam. If you can't answer a question, then carefully re-read the preceding chapter and, if necessary, refer to the previous books in this series.

When answering questions that involve writing scales in notation, you can write them in either the treble or bass clef. Either way, you need only write them ascending using whole notes.

Q1. Use letter names to write out the notes of the F# harmonic minor scale.

A1. _____

Q2. Use letter names to write out the notes of the pentatonic minor scale that has three flats in the key signature.

A2. _____

Q3. Write out the *scale spelling* for the harmonic minor scale.

A3. _____

Q4. Using the correct key signature and appropriate accidentals, write one octave of the E♭ blues scale, using either the treble or bass clef.

A4. _____

Q5. Using the correct key signature, write one octave of the A pentatonic major scale, using either the treble or bass clef.

A5. _____

Section Two – chords

In this section of the exam you may be asked to write out and identify any of the following chords built from major and natural minor scales within a range of keys to 3 sharps and 3 flats:

- Major, minor and diminished triads;
- Major 7th, minor 7th, dominant 7th and minor 7th ♭5 chords;
- Sus 2 and Sus 4 chords, 5th 'power' chords.

So that the chords learnt in theory can be used effectively in a practical way, you should be able to do the following:

- Use *chord symbols* to identify the chords.
- Write out, or identify, the *letter names* that make up each chord.
- Write out, or identify, each chord in standard *music notation*. You can write your answers in either the treble clef or the bass clef.
- Write out, or identify, the *chord spelling* of each chord and name the *intervals* between the root and each chord tone.

the theory

building chords

Chords are usually created by taking alternate notes from a scale. Any note in a scale can be used as the root (the first note) of a chord and so chords can be built on each degree of a scale.

The technical names of the notes in a chord are the root, the third, the fifth and the seventh.

The four chord types that can be built by taking alternate notes from a major or natural minor scale are:

- The major 7th chord
- The minor 7th chord
- The dominant 7th chord
- The minor 7th ♭5 chord

The minor 7th ♭5 chord is created by building a chord on either the seventh degree of a major scale or the second degree of a natural minor scale. It is also known as a *half-diminished* chord.

Here is the scale of C major with the chords that can be built on each degree:

C major scale	chord	degree	chord tones
<u>C</u> D <u>E</u> F <u>G</u> A <u>B</u>	Cmaj7	I	C E G B
C <u>D</u> E <u>F</u> G <u>A</u> B	Dm7	II	D F A C
C <u>D</u> E <u>F</u> G <u>A</u> B	Em7	III	E G B D
C D <u>E</u> <u>F</u> G <u>A</u> B	Fmaj7	IV	F A C E
C D E <u>F</u> <u>G</u> A B	G7	V	G B D F
<u>C</u> D E F <u>G</u> <u>A</u> B	Am7	VI	A C E G
C <u>D</u> E <u>F</u> G <u>A</u> <u>B</u>	Bm7♭5	VII	B D F A

All major keys have this pattern of chords. Notice that the chords on the 1st and 4th degrees are major 7th chords, the chords on the 2nd, 3rd and 6th degrees are minor 7th chords, the chord on the 5th degree is a dominant 7th chord, and the chord on the 7th degree is a minor 7th ♭5 chord (also known as a *half-diminished* chord).

Below are all these chords as they occur in the keys of C, G, D, A, F, B♭ and E♭ major.

Scale/Degree:	I	II	III	IV	V	VI	VII
C major:	Cmaj7	Dm7	Em7	Fmaj7	G7	Am7	Bm7♭5
G major:	Gmaj7	Am7	Bm7	Cmaj7	D7	Em7	F#m7♭5
D major:	Dmaj7	Em7	F#m7	Gmaj7	A7	Bm7	C#m7♭5
A major:	Amaj7	Bm7	C#m7	Dmaj7	E7	F#m7	G#m7♭5
F major:	Fmaj7	Gm7	Am7	B♭maj7	C7	Dm7	Em7♭5
B♭ major:	B♭maj7	Cm7	Dm7	E♭maj7	F7	Gm7	Am7♭5
E♭ major:	E♭maj7	Fm7	Gm7	A♭maj7	B♭7	Cm7	Dm7♭5

Here is the scale of A natural minor, with the chords that can be built on each degree:

A natural minor scale	chord	degree	chord tones
A B C D E F G	Am7	I	A C E G
A B C D E F G	Bm7♭5	II	B D F A
A B C D E F G	Cmaj7	III	C E G B
A B C D E F G	Dm7	IV	D F A C
A B C D E F G	Em7	V	E G B D
A B C D E F G	Fmaj7	VI	F A C E
A B C D E F G	G7	VII	G B D F

All natural minor keys have this pattern of chords. Notice that the chords on the 1st, 4th and 5th degrees are minor 7th chords, the chords on the 3rd and 6th degrees are major 7th chords, the chord on the 7th degree is a dominant 7th chord and the chord on the 2nd degree is a minor 7th ♭5 chord.

Below are these chords built from the A, E, B, F#, D, G and C natural minor scales.

Scale/Degree:	I	II	III	IV	V	VI	VII
A minor:	Am7	Bm7♭5	Cmaj7	Dm7	Em7	Fmaj7	G7
E minor:	Em7	F#m7♭5	Gmaj7	Am7	Bm7	Cmaj7	D7
B minor:	Bm7	C#m7♭5	Dmaj7	Em7	F#m7	Gmaj7	A7
F# minor:	F#m7	G#m7♭5	Amaj7	Bm7	C#m7	Dmaj7	E7
D minor:	Dm7	Em7♭5	Fmaj7	Gm7	Am7	B♭maj7	C7
G minor:	Gm7	Am7♭5	B♭maj7	Cm7	Dm7	E♭maj7	F7
C minor:	Cm7	Dm7♭5	E♭maj7	Fm7	Gm7	A♭maj7	B♭7

chord symbols

Here are the chord symbols for the four types of seventh chord, using C as the root of each chord. The chord symbols shown in the middle column are those most commonly used (and those recommended for use in the exam). A range of alternative symbols are sometimes used by pop musicians – these are shown in the right hand column.

Major seventh chord	Cmaj7	Cma7 CM7 C△ C△7
Minor seventh chord	Cm7	Cmi7 Cmin7 C-7
Dominant seventh chord	C7	Cdom7
Minor seventh ♭5 chord (also known as a half-diminished chord)	Cm7♭5	C-7♭5 Cø

chord tones

Here are the chord tones of the chords that have been added for the Grade Four exam. All the other major, minor and dominant 7th chords required for the exam have been covered in previous books in this series.

Major 7th chords				
A major:	A	C#	E	G#
E♭ maj7:	E♭	G	B♭	D
A♭ maj7:	A♭	C	E♭	G

Minor 7th chords				
F#m7:	F#	A	C#	E
C#m7:	C#	E	G#	B
Cm7:	C	E♭	G	B♭
Fm7:	F	A♭	C	E♭

Dominant 7th chords				
E7:	E	G#	B	D
B♭7:	B♭	D	F	A♭

Minor 7th ♭5 chords				
Bm7♭5:	B	D	F	A
F#m7♭5:	F#	A	C	E
C#m7♭5:	C#	E	G	B
G#m7♭5:	G#	B	D	F#
Em7♭5:	E	G	B♭	D
Am7♭5:	A	C	E♭	G
Dm7♭5:	D	F	A♭	C

chord notation

Here are the same chords written out using notation, in both the treble clef and the bass clef:

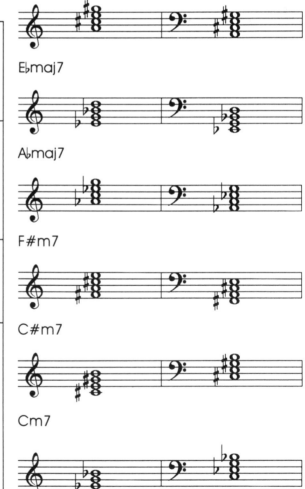

Amaj7

E♭maj7

A♭maj7

F#m7

C#m7

Cm7

Fm7

E7

Bb7

Bm7b5

F#m7b5

C#m7b5

G#m7b5

Em7b5

Am7b5

Dm7b5

other chord types

There are three other chord types that are set for the Grade Four exam.

Suspended chords

There are two types of suspended chords: the suspended 4th (sus4) chord and the suspended 2nd (sus2) chord.

In a sus4 chord the third is replaced by the fourth note of the major scale (with the same starting pitch). For example:

C major scale									Csus4		
C	D	E	F	G	A	B	C		C	F	G
1	2	3	4	5	6	7	8		1	4	5

In a sus2 chord the third is replaced by the second note of the major scale (with the same starting pitch). For example:

C major scale									Csus2		
C	D	E	F	G	A	B	C		C	D	G
1	2	3	4	5	6	7	8		1	2	5

Other chords can also be changed into sus chords. In particular, dominant 7th chords are often played as 7sus4 chords. This is done by replacing the 3rd note of the chord with the fourth note of the major scale with the same starting note. For example, C7sus4 contains the notes C F G Bb.

5th 'power chords'

5th 'power chords' are another chord type which have no third. In fact a 5th 'power chord' is made up of just the root and fifth, although the root is often doubled an octave higher to give a stonger sound. For example:

C major scale									C 5th 'power'		
C	D	E	F	G	A	B	C		C	G	C
1	2	3	4	5	6	7	8		1	5	8

In the exam you will be expected to include the octave when you write the notes of a 5th 'power chord'.

As with suspended chords, a 5th 'power chord' is not defined as either major or minor as there is no third. This type of chord is often played on electric guitar, where the sound of the chord is filled out by the use of distortion effects. 5th 'power chords' are played on any degree of the scale and also on *non-diatonic* scale notes – i.e. on notes which do not come from the scale.

<u>Chord symbols</u>

Here are some examples of how suspended chords and 5th 'power' chords are written using chord symbols.

Suspended 4th chord:	Csus4
Suspended 2nd chord:	Csus2
5th 'power chord':	C5

<u>Chord tones</u>

Here are some examples of the notes within suspended chords and 5th 'power' chords.

sus chords			
Csus4:	C	F	G
Csus2:	C	D	G
Asus4:	A	D	E
Asus2:	A	B	E
E♭sus4:	E♭	A♭	B♭
E♭sus2:	E♭	F	B♭

5th 'power chords'			
C5:	C	G	C
A5:	A	E	A
E♭5:	E♭	B♭	E♭

<u>Chord notation</u>

There follows some examples of how suspended chords and 5th 'power' chords are written using standard notation.

Csus4

Csus2

Asus4

Asus2
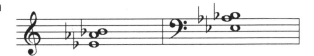

E♭sus4

E♭sus2

C5

A5

E♭5

chord spellings

In the same way that pop musicians often use numbers to talk about the notes in a scale, they also use numbers to talk about the notes in a chord. This is called the *chord spelling*. Each note in the chord is given a number, which refers to the *interval* between that note and the root of the chord.

All major 7th, minor 7th, dominant 7th and minor 7th ♭5 chords are constructed using a root, third, fifth and seventh.

For example, E♭ major 7th is numbered like this:

E♭	G	B♭	D
1	3	5	7

Rather than talking about the B♭ note in the E♭ major 7th chord, pop musicians might refer to it as the 5th of the chord.

Each type of chord has a unique chord spelling which enables easy comparison between different chord types.

Major 7th chords are numbered like this:

| 1 | 3 | 5 | 7 |

This is because the intervals from the root to the third, fifth and seventh notes in a major 7th chord, are the same size as the corresponding intervals from the keynote to the third, fifth and seventh notes in a major scale.

In a major chord or scale, the interval between the root and third is known as a *major third*, the interval between the root and the fifth is known as a *perfect fifth* and the interval between the root and the seventh is known as a *major seventh*.

This means that major 7th chords have a *major third* interval, between the root and the third note, a *perfect fifth* interval between the root and the fifth note and a *major seventh* interval between the root and the seventh note.

All other chord types are numbered, and the intervals named, in comparison to the major 7th chord (or major scale).

Minor 7th chords are numbered like this:

| 1 | ♭3 | 5 | ♭7 |

This means that minor 7th chords have a *flattened* (i.e. *minor*) *third* interval, between the root and the third note, a *perfect fifth* interval between the root and the fifth note and a *flattened* (i.e. *minor*) *seventh* interval between the root and the seventh note.

Dominant 7th chords are numbered like this:

| 1 | 3 | 5 | ♭7 |

This means that the dominant 7th chord has a *major third* interval, between the root and the third note, a *perfect fifth* interval between the root and the fifth note and a *flattened* (i.e. *minor*) *seventh* interval, between the root and the seventh note.

Minor 7th ♭5 chords are numbered like this:

| 1 | ♭3 | ♭5 | ♭7 |

This means that minor 7th ♭5 chords have a *flattened* (i.e. *minor*) *third* interval between the root and the third note, a *flattened* (i.e. *diminished*) *fifth* interval between the root and the fifth note, and a *flattened* (i.e. *minor*) interval between the root and the seventh note.

Note that an interval that is one half step smaller than a *major* interval is called a *flattened* (or *minor*) interval, whilst an interval that is one half step smaller than a *perfect* interval is called a *flattened* (or *diminished*) interval.

There follows a brief explanation as to why minor 7th, dominant 7th and minor 7th ♭5 chords are numbered in this way. In the exam, however, you will only be asked to identify, or write out the chord spelling and give the names of the intervals between the root and the chord tones of the chords listed.

Any chord which contains a *flattened* or *diminished* interval has a flat sign before the number in the chord spelling because the interval is one half step smaller than the corresponding interval in a major chord or scale.

For example, between C and E (root and 3rd in Cmaj7) there are four half steps, whilst between C and Eb (root and 3rd in Cm7) there are only three half steps. Consequently, the third in a minor 7th (or minor 7th b5 chord) is called a flattened 3rd (b3) or minor 3rd. For similar reasons, the seventh in a minor 7th, minor 7th b5 and dominant 7th chord is a called a flattened 7th (b7) or minor 7th, and the fifth in a minor 7th b5 chord is known as a flattened 5th (b5) or diminished 5th.

Suspended 4th chords are numbered like this:

```
1 4 5
```

This means that sus4 chords have a *perfect fourth* interval between the root and fourth note, and a *perfect fifth* interval between the root and the fifth note.

If a sus chord has a seventh added it would be numbered in a similar way. For example, a dominant 7sus4 chord would be numbered 1 4 5 b7

Suspended 2nd chords are numbered like this:

```
1 2 5
```

This means that sus2 chords have a *major second* interval between the root and second note, and a *perfect fifth* interval between the root and the fifth note.

5th 'power chords' are numbered like this:

```
1 5 8
```

This is because they use the root and fifth notes, and normally include the root doubled an octave higher.

comparing chords

You can use your knowledge of major chords and chord spellings to work out the notes contained in all other chords. For example, by knowing which notes are contained in the Dmaj7 chord it is possible to work out which notes are contained in the Dm7, D7, Dm7b5, Dsus4, Dsus2 and D5 chords:

major 7th chord:	1	3	5	7
Dmaj7:	D	F#	A	C#
minor 7th chord:	1	b3	5	b7
Dm7:	D	F	A	C
dominant 7th chord:	1	3	5	b7
D7:	D	F#	A	C
minor 7th b5 chord:	1	b3	b5	b7
Dm7b5:	D	F	Ab	C
sus 4 chord:	1	4	5	
Dsus4:	D	G	A	
sus 2 chord:	1	2	5	
Dsus2:	D	E	A	
5th 'power chord':	1	5	8	
D5:	D	A	D	

Alternatively, chords can also be compared directly with each other (without reference to the major 7th chord). For example:

- a minor 7th chord only differs from a dominant 7th in that the third is a minor, not a major, third interval from the root.

- a minor 7th b5 chord only differs from a minor 7th chord in that the fifth is a flattened, not a perfect, fifth interval from the root.

- A 5th 'power chord' only differs from a major triad in that the third note is removed and the note an octave above the root is added.

working out chords

All of the chords in this section of the exam are derived from the major and natural minor scales in Section One. Many of the major 7th and minor 7th chords are built on the keynote of one of these major or natural minor scales. However, some of the major 7th and minor 7th chords, and all of the dominant 7th and minor 7th ♭5 chords, are built on degrees of the scale other than the first degree.

You can work out the notes in all of the required chords in the following ways.

Major 7th chords.

Because major 7th chords occur on the 1st, and 4th degrees of the major scale, you need to identify a major scale in which the root note of the chord occurs on either of these two degrees. Then, take four alternate notes (the 1st, 3rd, 5th and 7th) starting from this degree of the scale to work out the notes in the chord. For example: by taking the 1st, 3rd, 5th and 7th notes of the E♭ major scale you will discover the notes in the E♭ major 7th chord (E♭, G, B♭ and D).

In all chords it is essential that you take account of any sharps or flats that arise in the key so that the correct enharmonic spelling is used.

Minor 7th chords.

Because minor 7th chords occur on the 2nd, 3rd and 6th degrees of the major scale, you need to identify a major scale in which the root note of the chord occurs on one of these degrees. Then, take four alternate notes starting from this degree of the scale to work out the notes in the chord.

Alternatively, just take the 1st, 3rd, 5th and 7th notes of the natural minor scale with the same starting note. For example: by taking the 1st, 3rd, 5th and 7th notes of the C natural minor scale you will discover the notes in the C minor 7th chord (C, E♭, G and B♭).

Dominant 7th chords.

Because dominant 7th chords occur on the 5th degree of the major scale, you need to identify a major scale in which the root note of the chord occurs on this degree. Then, take four alternate notes starting from this degree of the scale to work out the notes in the chord. For example, the E dominant 7th chord is built from the fifth degree of the A major scale – taking the E, G#, B and D notes from this scale.

Minor 7♭5 chords.

Because minor 7♭5 chords occur on the 7th degree of the major scale, you need to identify a major scale in which the root note of the chord occurs on this degree. Then, take four alternate notes starting from this degree of the scale to work out the notes in the chord. For example, B occurs on the 7th degree of the C major scale, therefore the notes in the B minor 7 ♭5 chord (B, D, F and A) are taken from this scale.

Sus4 and sus2 chords.

These can be considered as variations of other chords. To work out a sus4 chord simply replace the 3rd of the original chord with the 4th note from the major scale with the same starting note. For example, by replacing the E note with an F note, the C major triad will become Csus4.

To work out a sus2 chord replace the 3rd of the original chord with the 2nd note of the major scale with the same starting note. For example, by replacing the E note with a D note, the C major triad will become Csus2.

5th 'power chords'.

These can be worked out by adding the notes a perfect fifth and an octave above the root note.

Alternatively, work out the notes of either a major or minor triad with the same root and then remove the 3rd of the chord and add the note an octave above the root. For example, if the E note is removed from the C major triad (and the octave added) it will become C5.

Below are some examples of the types of questions that candidates may be asked in this section of the exam. If you can't answer a question, then carefully re-read the preceding chapter and, if necessary, refer to the previous books in this series.

When answering questions that involve writing chords in notation, you can write your answers in either the treble clef or the bass clef. You should place the notes of each chord vertically on top of one another using whole notes. The notes of each chord should be written in *root position* – starting with the root note at the bottom and progressing in order to the highest note.

Q1. Using letter names write the notes of the A5 'power chord'.

Q2. Which chord contains the notes: D G A?

Q3. Write out the chord spelling for the minor 7th ♭5 chord.

Q4. Name two types of chord which do not contain a third.

Q5. In the D7 chord, what is the interval between the root note and C.

Q6. Write the notes of the B♭7 chord in either the treble or bass clef.

Section Three – rhythm notation

In this section of the exam you will be asked to use some of the following note and rest values in $\frac{4}{4}$ $\frac{3}{4}$ $\frac{2}{4}$ or $\frac{6}{8}$ time.

- whole notes (semibreves)
- whole rests (semibreve rests)
- half notes (minims)
- half rests (minim rests)
- quarter notes (crotchets)
- quarter rests (crotchet rests)
- eighth notes (quavers)
- eighth rests (quaver rests)
- sixteenth notes (semiquavers)
- sixteenth rests (semiquaver rests)
- dotted notes and rests (for all of the above, where appropriate, except for sixteenth notes)
- tied notes

So that the rhythm notation learnt in theory can be used effectively in a practical way, you should be able to do the following:

- Group notes and rests correctly within $\frac{4}{4}$ $\frac{3}{4}$ $\frac{2}{4}$ or $\frac{6}{8}$ time.
- Compose simple rhythms in $\frac{4}{4}$ $\frac{3}{4}$ $\frac{2}{4}$ or $\frac{6}{8}$ time, using the note and rest values listed.

the theory

The basics of rhythm notation are covered in the earlier books in this series and you should refer to these books if you are unsure of any of the terms and concepts mentioned below. This chapter concentrates on the topics which have been added at this grade – in particular, *tied notes*.

tied notes

A tie is used to 'join together' two notes of the same pitch, to increase the duration of the note.

In the above example, the D note would be held for the equivalent of five eighth notes. It is not possible to use a dot after the initial

D as this would increase the duration of the note to the equivalent of six eighth notes.

Another common instance where ties are used is across bar lines, to enable a note to last beyond the end of a bar.

In the above example, a tie has to be used so that the C note at the end of bar 1 can sound for three beats.

Ties can be used to join any number of notes of the same pitch. In the following example, the D note is only sounded once but lasts for 16 beats.

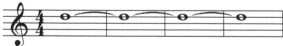

Tied notes can be used in both simple and compound time signatures.

Rests are not tied together: because they are silent there would be no point in doing so!

Except for when a note lasts beyond a barline, dotted notes are generally used in preference to ties. However, sometimes it is preferable to use a tie in order to show where a beat falls. For instance, in the following example, the first bar is easier to read than the second bar because the tie indicates where the main beats of the bar lie.

time signatures

$\frac{2}{4}$, $\frac{3}{4}$ and $\frac{4}{4}$ are all known as *simple time*. In these time signatures each beat is represented by a quarter note which can be divided into two.

$\frac{6}{8}$ time is known as *compound time*. Although in $\frac{6}{8}$ time there is an equivalent of six eighth notes in a bar, there are only two main beats: two dotted quarter notes – each comprising three eighth note pulses. So in $\frac{6}{8}$ time, each of its two beats can be divided into three.

In simple time signatures the upper figure represents the number of beats per bar, whereas in $\frac{6}{8}$ time the upper number represents the number of pulses in the bar (which is three times the number of beats in the bar).

grouping of notes and rests

There are certain rules about how notes and rests can be grouped. These exist in music notation so that all the beats of the bar can be clearly identified, and consequently the written music is easier to read.

At this level you should be aware of the following rules and the exceptions to these rules.

RULE 1

Quarter notes, and notes shorter than a quarter note, are beamed together when they belong to one beat.

For example:

Exceptions

i) In a bar of $\frac{4}{4}$ time, you can beam together all eighth and sixteenth notes that are in the first half of a bar (beats one and two) or in the second half of the bar (beats three and four). However, you should not beam together notes across the middle of the bar (beats two and three).

ii) In $\frac{2}{4}$ and $\frac{3}{4}$ time you can beam together all eighth and sixteenth notes within a bar.

For example:

RULE 2

When you write rests, each beat and each half beat must be completed with the appropriate rests. This is because it is much easier to read music if you can clearly see where each beat and each half beat starts.

For example:

Exceptions

i) In a bar of $\frac{4}{4}$ time you can write a half (minim) rest in the first half of the bar (beats one and two) or in the second half of the bar (beats three and four). However, you should not write a half rest in the middle of the bar (beats two and three) – instead you should use two quarter (crotchet) rests.

ii) The whole note (semibreve) rest (also known as the 'whole bar' rest), indicates a whole bar rest in all popular time signatures, including $\frac{2}{4}$ and $\frac{3}{4}$. Consequently, dotted half note rests are not used in $\frac{3}{4}$; a whole bar rest is used instead.

iii) Although it is normally easier to see all the main beats if you write rests out in full (with each beat having a rest of its own where needed), you can use dotted rests in certain places (such as at the start of a bar in $\frac{4}{4}$ time).

For example:

Both of these bars are acceptable.

This bar is *incorrect* because the rest starts midway through beat 1.

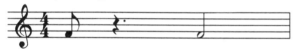

compound time signatures

RULE 1

Notes shorter than a dotted quarter note should be grouped together when they belong to one beat. This helps to clarify where the underlying dotted quarter note beat is.

For example, in $\frac{6}{8}$ time the first three eighth notes (including any combination of eighth notes and sixteenth notes) should be beamed together. Similarly, the last three eighth notes should be beamed together.

This is correct

This bar is *incorrect* because although it contains the same order of notes as the example above, the notes are grouped as though in $\frac{3}{4}$ time.

RULE 2

The same rule for writing rests in simple time – that each beat must be completed with the appropriate rests – applies in compound time. When you write rests in compound time you must remember that each beat is equivalent to a dotted quarter note.

This is correct.

This is *incorrect* because it is written as though in $\frac{3}{4}$ time.

Exception

The whole note (semibreve) rest indicates a whole bar rest in all popular time signatures, including compound time signatures. Consequently, dotted half note rests are not used in $\frac{6}{8}$ time as a whole bar rest is used instead.

There are specific additional rules about how the rests within each beat can be written. Remember, a beat in compound time lasts for a dotted quarter note.

- If the first two eighth notes of a beat are silent, a single quarter note rest should be used.

- If the last two eighth notes of a beat are silent, then two eighth note rests (rather than a single quarter note rest) should be used.

Distinguishing between $\frac{6}{8}$ and $\frac{3}{4}$

As both $\frac{6}{8}$ and $\frac{3}{4}$ time can contain six eighth notes, it is important to group them correctly. In $\frac{6}{8}$ time there should always be a split between the 3rd and 4th eighth notes (because in $\frac{6}{8}$ the beat is divided into two groups of three eighth notes).

Both lines of music below have the same note values, but notice how the grouping changes according to the time signature used.

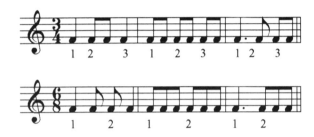

the exam

Below are some examples of the types of questions that candidates may be asked in this section of the exam. If you can't answer a question, then carefully re-read the preceding chapter and, if necessary, consult the earlier books in this series.

Q1. Complete the following bars by adding the appropriate rest or rests in the spaces marked *.

A1.

Q2. Re-write the following bar correctly.

A2.

Q3. Re-write the following bar correctly.

A3.

Q4. At a pitch of you choice, write a four bar rhythm in ²⁄₄ time, using a combination of dotted quarter notes (dotted crotchets), quarter notes (crotchets), eighth notes (quavers), sixteenth notes (semiquavers) and at least two ties. Use either the treble or bass clef.

A4.

Section Four – popular music

There are three areas of popular music that candidates will be asked questions on in this section of the exam.

- influential bands, vocalists and instrumentalists

- commonly used instruments

- commonly used performance directions

influential artists

So that you increase your general knowledge of the recording artists and performers who have had the greatest influence on the development of popular music, at this grade you will be asked questions about the following:

- Bob Dylan
- The Sex Pistols
- Bob Marley
- Pink Floyd

You may be asked to name:

- Some of their hit recordings.

- Some of the bands they have played or sung with.

- The instruments played by instrumentalists.

- The period during which they performed or recorded.

- The styles of music with which they are associated.

Below is a short profile of each group or performer, giving all the information you need to know for the Grade Four exam. We recommend, that as well as reading these profiles, you also listen to some of their recordings.

Bob Dylan

American-born, singer/songwriter, Bob Dylan is one of the most important artists in the history of popular music. During the 1960s, his song-writing about the social issues of the period played a core role in popularising folk music and in fusing it with other popular music styles.

Dylan originally began as a folk singer/guitarist and harmonica player. He was influenced by folk legend Woody Guthrie, and his first four albums are purely in a folk idiom, and include classic tracks such as *Blowin' In The Wind* and *Don't Think Twice It's All Right*. The fourth album, *The Times They Are A' Changin'*, released in 1964, was Dylan's most successful in terms of sales. Many of his early songs contained a strong social protest theme, although his next album, *Another Side of Bob Dylan* (also recorded in 1964) consisted of songs inspired more by personal reflective material and was an indication that he would not always stay a folk/protest singer. In 1965, inspired by the success of bands like The Beatles, he recorded the highly successful *Highway 61 Revisited* 'electric' album, which included the classic track *Like A Rolling Stone* (which reached number two in the American charts). Once he began working with contemporary electric backing group *The Band*, Dylan's music blended expressionistic and poetic lyrics with rock, pop, R'n'B and blues inspired music. In doing so, he broadened the boundaries of popular music. This amalgam of styles disillusioned some of his initial folk fan base, but his music reached a broader audience.

Dylan has recorded over 40 albums, encompassing a wide range of styles (including a born-again Christian theme from the late 1970s onwards). Although the quality of his performances can be erratic, Dylan has a large and dedicated following and (at the time of writing) he still undertakes regular concert tours. Many of his songs are regularly performed by other artists, and cover versions of his songs have been recorded by a multitude of artists in a vast range of styles.

Some of his most famous recordings are:

- *Blowin' In The Wind*
- *Subterranean Homesick Blues*
- *Hurricane*

- *Mr Tambourine Man*
- *Like A Rolling Stone*
- *Knockin' On Heaven's Door*

The Sex Pistols

The British group the Sex Pistols was a short-lived but immensely influential band which, in the 1970s, helped to create punk rock. In response to the increasingly sophisticated 'progressive' rock music of the time, the Sex Pistols, together with the marketing by their manager Malcolm McLaren, created a type of music that focused on energy and attitude, rather than technical musical ability. Punk opened the way for many people with musical ideas, but limited technical ability on their instruments, to form groups and record their music. Many styles of popular music, such as *grunge, indie, thrash metal* and even *rap* owe their foundations to the legacy of ground breaking punk bands – of which the Sex Pistols was the most prominent.

The group members consisted of:

- Johnny Rotten (John Lydon) – vocals
- Steve Jones – guitar
- Paul Cook – drums
- Glen Matlock – bass
  (replaced by Sid Vicious in 1977)

The group signed to a major record label, EMI, but the outrageous behaviour of the group members at gigs and on television caused EMI to drop the group without releasing a record. The publicity that they received, however, ensured that the Sex Pistols quickly became a household name.

The Sex Pistol's first album was released in the UK in 1977 and went straight to number one – despite not being allowed to be played on the radio, advertised on TV or stocked in record shops. The album was also distributed in the USA, where it initially achieved a cult following rather than reaching a mainstream audience. The group folded in the autumn of 1978 having only released one album.

Some of the most famous tracks are:

- *Anarchy In The UK*
- *God Save The Queen*
- *Pretty Vacant*
- *Holidays In The Sun*

Johnny Rotten of the Sex Pistols

Bob Marley

Jamaican born, singer/songwriter and guitarist, Bob Marley was the leading member of the reggae group Bob Marley and The Wailers which was the first reggae group to make a serious impact on the mainstream popular music market. Although Marley had made many recordings during the 1960s, his first major success was with the Wailers album *Catch A Fire* which made its way into the UK charts in 1973 with a band line up of:

- Bob Marley – vocals, guitar
- Bunny Wailer – vocals, percussion
- Peter Tosh – vocals, guitar, keyboards
- Aston Barrett – bass
- Carlton Barrett – drums
- Earl Lindo – organ

In 1974 both Bunny Wailer and Peter Tosh left to pursue solo careers. Their replacements included three female vocalists – known as the I-Threes. This gave the music a gospel / soul flavour and by doing so made it more accessible to popular music audiences of the time. By 1976 Marley had achieved widespread success and had brought the influence of reggae music into many forms of popular music. By the time of his death in 1981, he had achieved international acclaim as a songwriter and musician.

Here are some of his most famous recordings:

- *Lively Up Yourself*
- *Exodus*
- *Could You Be Loved*
- *Stir It Up*
- *No Woman No Cry*
- *One Love*

Pink Floyd

The British band Pink Floyd, which was formed in 1965, was originally an underground 'art' band, playing a mixture of psychedelic rock, progressive jazz and electronic music. The members of the band were:

- Syd Barrett – lead guitar/vocals (replaced by Dave Gilmour in 1968)
- Roger Waters – bass/vocals
- Rick Wright – keyboards
- Nick Mason – drums

Barrett who was an art student, provided most of the material, while the other three (all architectural students) were proficient musicians. The members of the band were all interested in the avant-garde and improvisation and this, together with Roger Waters' interest in electronics meant that their concerts became audio-visual extravaganzas: featuring extended versions of their songs, light shows and state-of-the-art amplification.

Their debut album, *The Piper At The Gates Of Dawn*, was one of the most innovative of the 1960s, as it developed the idea of the 'concept album'.

Syd Barrett, who wrote most of the material for this album, became ill and in 1968 was replaced by Dave Gilmour. The band continued to record and perform, and in 1973 produced *Dark Side of the Moon* – one of the best-selling albums of all time. (It remained in the billboard charts until 1988; a total of over 700 consecutive weeks). The next three albums, *Wish You Were Here*, *Animals* and *The Wall* each took two years to record, but firmly established Pink Floyd as the premier progressive and experimental rock band of the period.

In 1981 Rick Wright left the band, and in 1983 Roger Waters also left, following the recording of the album *The Final Cut*. Wright then rejoined, and despite being sued by Waters for use of the name, Pink Floyd continued to undertake epic concert tours and record successful albums, such as *A Momentary Lapse of Reason* and *The Division Bell*.

Some of their most famous recordings are:

- See *Emily Play*
- *Money*
- *Interstellar Overdrive*
- *Comfortably Numb*
- *Shine On You Crazy Diamond*
- *Another Brick In The Wall*

instruments

So that you have a knowledge of the instruments that are commonly used in popular music, you may be asked questions about the following instruments:

- electric and acoustic guitars
- bass guitars
- keyboards
- drum kit
- saxophones
- brass instruments

Below is a description of each of the instruments – giving all the information you need to know about each instrument for the Grade Four exam. We recommend that you try to hear each of the instruments being played – either live, or at least, on a recording.

electric and acoustic guitars

- Standard electric and acoustic guitars are normally made of wood and have six steel strings. Nylon strung acoustic guitars also exist, but these are more widely used in classical than in popular music.

- The strings on a standard guitar are normally tuned to E, A, D, G, B and E, starting from the lowest string. There are two octaves between the two E strings. Different notes are produced through changing the length of a string by the player pressing on different places on the fingerboard of the guitar. The fingerboard is divided into half steps (semitones), by the use of metal frets.

- Although the strings can be picked with the fingers, normally in popular music a small plastic device known as a *plectrum* (or *pick*) is used to strike the strings, which can be played simultaneously to create chords or individually for single-note lead playing.

- On electric guitars the sound is produced by the vibration of the steel strings being electrically 'picked up' by an in-built device called a *pick up* and then amplified. On acoustic guitars the sound is also produced by the vibration of the strings, but with the hollow body of the guitar amplifying the sound.

- An electric guitar needs to be played through an *amplifier* and *speaker* in order to be heard. The term *amp* can refer to an amplifier and speaker contained in one unit, or a unit which contains only an amplifier. In the latter case, a separate unit containing a speaker is needed. This is often referred to as a *cab* (short for speaker cabinet).

The distinctive sound of an electric guitar is created by the interaction of the guitar, amplifier and speaker. In addition, various electronic effects can be wired-in to create a wide range of different sounds. Some standard guitar effects are:

a) distortion (overdrive)

b) reverb and echo (delay)

c) chorus

d) wah-wah

e) phaser

■ Although acoustic guitars can be played without amplification, they usually require amplification during performances in order to match the volume of other instruments. Acoustic guitars can be amplified by placing a microphone in front of the 'sound-hole' of the guitar, or by attaching a *pick up*.

A guitarist has two main functions in popular music:

1) To play *rhythm guitar*. Rhythm guitar parts often consist of chords played in repeated rhythmic patterns that link with the bass and drum parts. In this context, the guitarist can be seen as part of 'the rhythm section'.

2) To play *lead guitar*. In this context, the guitar is a *lead* or *soloing* instrument. Lead guitar parts are sometimes pre-prepared riffs or melodies, but solos are often *improvised*. The majority of lead guitar uses single note playing, although it can sometimes incorporate *double stops* or chords.

bass guitars

■ A standard bass guitar is usually made of wood and is a similar shape (but slightly larger size) to an electric guitar. The standard bass guitar has four strings that, starting from the lowest string, are tuned to E, A, D and G – an octave lower than standard guitar strings. Different

notes are produced through changing the length of a string by the player pressing on different places on the fingerboard of the bass guitar. The fingerboard is normally divided into half steps (semitones), by the use of metal frets, although, some players use *fretless* basses to enable them to *slide* between notes more easily.

■ In recent years, five string basses (which have an extra B string added below the E string) have become increasingly used in some forms of popular music. Occasionally, six string basses (where in addition to the B string, a C string is added above the G string) are also used by some players.

■ Bass strings are normally picked with the fingers, although some players prefer to use a *plectrum*. Although some chords can be played on the bass guitar, most bass parts are single-note lines.

■ The sound of a bass guitar is produced by the vibration of the steel strings being electrically 'picked up' by the instrument's in-built *pick up* and then amplified. Bass amplifiers and speakers have different specifications in comparison to guitar amplifiers, as they are built to reproduce the lower frequency range of the bass guitar.

■ Electronic effects units (such as compression, chorus, octaver and phaser) can be connected between the bass and the amplifier, but usually bass guitars are played without effects.

The fundamental role of the bass player is to be the link between the rhythm stated by the drums and the harmony stated by the guitar or keyboard.

keyboards

- Although pianos are the most traditional of all modern keyboard instruments, in contemporary popular music electric pianos, electronic keyboards and synthesisers are more commonly used. Collectively, these are known as *keyboards*.

- Keyboards are made in many different sizes, but the notes are always laid out like a piano – with the white keys producing the natural notes (C D E F G A B) and the black keys producing the flats and sharps.

- The keys on pianos and on good quality keyboards are *touch sensitive*. This means that the keys respond to how hard or softly the player touches them and enables the player to play with greater expression. Some electric keyboards also have *weighted* keys, to re-create the feel of a piano.

- Pianos have foot pedals attached that enable the player to either strengthen and sustain notes, or to soften and mute notes. Some keyboards also have similar pedals, particularly a sustain or volume pedal.

- Keyboards usually have a variety of in-built piano and organ sounds, as well as a wide range of other *instrumental* sounds which re-create the sound of specific instruments. *Sampled* sounds (where real instruments have been digitally recorded) are usually more realistic than *synthesised* sounds, which are created electronically. Keyboards can also have many unique *synthesised*

sounds, which do not emulate the sound of traditional instruments, and can be interesting musical sounds in their own right.

- The keys on many keyboards can be split into different sections and assigned to different sounds to allow the player to play, for example, a bass part and chords, or string and brass sounds.

- Many electronic keyboards have small in-built amplifiers and speakers, but for live performances they need to be amplified to achieve sufficient volume.

Keyboard players can fulfil several roles.

1) To be part of the rhythm section: adding to the rhythms created by the bass, drums and guitar – as well as stating the harmony by playing chords. They might also play an additional bass part.

2) To play lead lines; both composed melodies and improvised solos.

3) (On electric keyboards). To play brass or string parts.

4) (On electric keyboards). To add texture by using *synth pads* (synthesised sounds which are used to fill out the sound – often in place of a string section).

drum kit

- A drum kit consists of various percussion instruments arranged together so that they can all be played by one person using both hands and both feet

- The drums shells themselves are made of wood, metal or synthetic materials, and are completed with *drum heads* (traditionally known as *skins*) made from plastic.

- Drums are usually played using wooden *drumsticks* (which sometimes have nylon tips). To achieve a different and quieter sound sometimes special *brushes* are used instead of sticks.

- The larger the size of the drum, the lower the pitch of the drum will be. The bass (or kick) drum is therefore the lowest pitched drum in a conventional kit.

- The pitch of a drum can be changed by *tuning* it. By increasing how tightly the skins are stretched over the drum, by using a *drum key*, the sound of the drum changes. The tighter the skin is stretched the higher the pitch will be. Drums are sometimes muted with taping or mufflers to reduce any unwanted overtones.

- The cymbals which complete the kit are made of metal – usually brass.

A standard drum kit is made up of the following:

a) *bass* (or *kick*) *drum* which is struck with a foot-operated pedal

b) *snare drum*

c) one or more high *tom toms* and a low (*floor*) *tom tom*;

d) *ride cymbal*

e) *crash cymbal*

f) pair of cymbals known as a *hi hat* (which can be closed or opened with a foot operated pedal).

The drummer is the foundation of the rhythm section. The drum pattern is used to establish the rhythmic style of the music and also to keep time. Drum accents and fills are used to emphasise certain points of the music.

saxophones

- There are different sizes of saxophone, but the two most commonly used in popular music are the *tenor saxophone* and the (higher pitched) *alto saxophone*. *Baritone saxophones*, which are low pitched compared to other saxophones, are sometimes used as part of a *horn section*. *Soprano saxophones*, which are high pitched compared to other saxophones, are sometimes used for lead solos.

- The body of the saxophone is hollow and made of brass. Air is blown through the body via the mouthpiece, where a *reed* (a small strip of cane) is attached. The reed vibrates producing sound waves which then resonate through the body of the saxophone. The mouthpieces are made out of either ebonite (rubber) or metal, both of which have a different sound quality.

- In a concert setting saxophones are usually amplified by using a microphone connected to a P.A. system.

In popular music saxophonists have two main roles:

1) as part of a 'horn section', playing backing riffs. A typical pop music horn section would consist of a trumpet, a tenor or alto saxophone and a trombone (although sometimes baritone saxophones are used instead of trombones).

2) as a solo instrument, playing both composed melodies and improvised solos.

brass instruments

- The most commonly used brass instruments in popular music are trumpets and trombones. Both instruments are made of brass.

- There are different sizes of trumpets, but the most commonly used ones are known as *Bb trumpets*.

- There are different sizes of trombone, but the most commonly used ones are the *tenor trombone* and the *bass trombone*. The tenor trombone is higher in pitch, and is more often used in popular music, than the bass trombone.

- The sound is produced in both instruments by air being blown through the instrument: the player's lips vibrate and create sound waves that are amplified by the body of the instrument. Different notes are produced by changing the amount of tension in the lips.

- Trumpets also have three *valves*, each of which, when pressed, changes the length of the tube and produces further notes.

- In trombones the length of the tube is changed, and further notes produced, by the use of a *slide*. There are also, lesser used, *valve trombones*, which operate in a similar way as trumpets.

- Trumpets and trombones use *mutes* to change the sound of the instrument. These are devices which are made out of metal, rubber or plastic and are held over the end of the instruments (where the sound comes out), muting the volume and changing the sound. Some of the different mutes used are:

  a) cup

  b) straight

  c) Harman

  d) plunger

  e) bucket

- In a concert setting, brass instruments are sometimes amplified using microphones and a P.A. system.

In popular music brass players have two main roles:

1) as part of a horn section, playing backing riffs. A typical pop music horn section would consist of a trumpet, a trombone and a tenor or alto saxophone.

2) as a solo instrument, playing both composed melodies and improvised solos.

musical signs and terminology

So that you have a good knowledge of the common musical signs and terminology used in popular music you will be asked questions on the following areas:

- tempo
- dynamics
- articulation
- directions for rests and repeats

So that the signs and terminology learnt in theory can be effectively used in a practical way, you should be able to:

- understand the practical differences in tempo between different bpm (metronome) markings

- explain in practical terms the meaning of different dynamic markings

- add dynamic markings to a chord progression or melody

- add articulation markings to a chord progression or melody

- understand and use directions for rests

- understand and use directions for repeated bars

- understand and use directions for repeated chords

- condense a chord progression using repeat marks and 1st and 2nd time section endings

- write out in full a chord progression that contains repeats and 1st and 2nd time section endings.

tempo

In popular music the most commonly used indication of tempo is to specify the *beats per minute* (*bpm*) – this is sometimes also referred to as the metronome marking.

For example:

$$\quarternote = 60$$

This means that there are 60 quarter note beats per minute.

$$\quarternote = 120$$

This means that there are 120 quarter note beats per minute, so a tempo of $\quarternote = 120$ bpm is twice as fast as a tempo of $\quarternote = 60$ bpm.

bpm can also be measured using other types of beat. For example:

$$\quarternote. = 60$$

This means that there are 60 dotted quarter note beats per minute.

dynamics

Below are the symbols used to indicate how quietly or loudly notes or phrases should be played:

symbol	meaning	Italian term
pp	very softly	pianissimo
p	softly	piano
mp	moderately softly	mezzo piano
mf	moderately strongly	mezzo forte
f	strongly	forte
ff	very strongly	fortissimo

You can add more *p*s or *f*s to instruct the performer to play extremely softly or extremely strongly.

To indicate that the music should gradually become louder or quieter, *hairpins* are used.

This hairpin indicates that you should start quietly and gradually get louder.

The term *crescendo* (or *cresc.*) is also used to indicate that you should gradually increase volume.

This hairpin indicates that you should start loudly and gradually get quieter.

The terms *decrescendo* (*decresc.*) or *diminuendo* (*dim.*) are also used to indicate that you should gradually reduce volume.

To be really precise you should also indicate the dynamic level at the start and finish of the hairpin. For example:

The following direction means that you should start moderately strongly and gradually play more quietly, until you are playing very softly by the end of the hairpin.

articulation

The following symbols tell you how to play each note.

A dot above or below the notehead tells you to play the note short – about half its length. This is known as a *staccato* dot.

A straight line above or below the notehead tells you to play the note to its full length and 'lean' on it slightly. This is known as a *tenuto* mark.

A 'V' lying on its side above a notehead means accent the note. These are called *accents*.

Slurs are used where notes should be played together as smoothly as possible. For example, saxophonists and brass instrumentalists will play all the slurred notes in one breath, without accenting any of them. Guitarists and bass players slur notes by 'hammering-on' or 'pulling-off' onto the notes with their fretting fingers, instead of picking the string again as normal for each new note.

The symbol ⌒ is called a *fermata* (although it is commonly referred to as a *pause* mark). It can be used with either notes, chords or rests, and indicates that the note, chord or rest is held for an extra (unspecified) amount of time. The length of the *pause* is decided by the performer.

directions for rests

A bar of rest is indicated by a whole (semibreve) rest. If there is more than one bar of rest, a horizontal line is written through the bar with the number of silent bars written above it.

This is much easier for a performer to count than eight separate bars containing whole rests.

directions for repeats

■ If one bar is to be repeated then the symbol ╱ can be used. This symbol can be repeated as necessary. It can be used to indicate repeated bars of chord symbols, as well as notation.

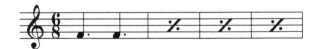

- If the phrase to be repeated is longer than one bar, a similar symbol is used but with the a double oblique line crossing the same number of bars as in the phrase, and with the number of bars written above it.

Remember this means that two bars are to be repeated once, not one bar played twice.

- If a chord is to be repeated within a bar, the repeats can be indicated by either slanted lines or dots.

For example:

This is very useful if there are two chords per bar and you wish to specify on which beat they change.

For example:

If the rhythms are not specified then the performer will assume that the chord changes half way through the bar.

- To indicate that a section of music should be repeated (played twice) *repeat marks* are used. A double bar line, followed by two dots either side of the middle line of the staff indicates the start of the section and two dots either side of the middle line of the staff, followed by a double bar line indicates the end of the section to be repeated. (If there are no dots at the start of the section, then repeat from the beginning of the piece).

Repeat marks can also be used in chord charts.

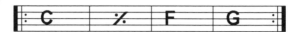

Any number of bars may be included within the repeat marks.

If the section is to be repeated more than once, the number of times it is to be played is written above the last repeat dots.

This means play the phrase four times in total.

- If two sections of music are identical, except for the last bar or bars, repeat marks are used in conjunction with *first time* and *second time ending* directions.

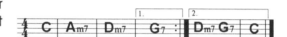

the exam

Below are some examples of the types of questions that candidates may be asked in this section of the exam. If you can't answer a question, then carefully re-read the preceding chapter.

Q1. Name three members of the Sex Pistols, stating the role of each one.

A1. _____

_____

Q2. What name was used by group of the three female backing vocalists in Bob Marley and The Wailers, and how did they change the sound of the The Wailers' music?

A2. _____

_____

Q3. Name two albums released in different decades by the band Pink Floyd, stating in which decade each was released.

A3. _____

Q4. Name two types of effects units that might be used with an electric guitar.

A4. _____

Q5. In popular music what are the two main functions for a brass player?

A5. _____

_____

Q6. How would you play a phrase if it had the following signs below it?

_pp_ ——————————— _mf_

A6. _____

_____

Q7. Condense the following chord progression using repeat marks and 1st and 2nd time ending directions.

```
|| C          | C          | F          | F          |
|  Em7        | Am7        | Dm7        | G7         |
|  C          | C          | F          | F          |
|  Em7        | Am7        | Dm7   G7   | C          ||
```

A7.

Section Five – harmony

In this section of the exam, within a range of keys up to and including three sharps and three flats, you will be asked to demonstrate your knowledge of:

- The patterns of major 7th, minor 7th, dominant 7th and minor 7th ♭5 chords built from major and natural minor scales;

- Constructing chord progressions, and constructing and identifying V – I (perfect) and IV – I (plagal) cadences, using chords built from major and natural minor scales;

- The application of major, pentatonic major, natural minor and pentatonic minor scales in improvisation.

So that the harmony learnt in theory can be used effectively in a practical way, you should be able to do the following:

- Write out, and identify, the patterns of chords in the keys specified.

- Write chord progressions in given keys.

- Identify and construct V – I (perfect) and IV – I (plagal) cadences.

- Identify which scale would be suitable to use for improvising over a given chord progression.

- Write chord progressions over which major, pentatonic major, natural minor or pentatonic minor scales could be used for improvising.

the theory

The type of seventh chord that can be built in thirds from each degree of a major scale is always the same for each particular scale degree, regardless of the key.

All major keys have the following pattern of chords:

I	II	III	IV	V	VI	VII
major 7th	minor 7th	minor 7th	major 7th	dominant 7th	minor 7th	minor 7th ♭5

Below are these chords built from the C, G, D, A, F, B♭ and E♭ major scales.

Degree:	I	II	III	IV	V	VI	VII
C major:	Cmaj7	Dm7	Em7	Fmaj7	G7	Am7	Bm7♭5
G major:	Gmaj7	Am7	Bm7	Cmaj7	D7	Em7	F#m7♭5
D major:	Dmaj7	Em7	F#m7	Gmaj7	A7	Bm7	C#m7♭5
A major:	Amaj7	Bm7	C#m7	Dmaj7	E7	F#m7	G#m7♭5
F major:	Fmaj7	Gm7	Am7	B♭maj7	C7	Dm7	Em7♭5
B♭ major:	B♭maj7	Cm7	Dm7	E♭maj7	F7	Gm7	Am7♭5
E♭ major:	E♭maj7	Fm7	Gm7	A♭maj7	B♭7	Cm7	Dm7♭5

Notice that the chords built on the 1st and 4th degrees are major 7th chords, the chords built on the 2nd, 3rd and 6th degrees are minor 7th chords, the chord built on the 5th degree is a dominant 7th chord and the chord built on the 7th degree is a minor 7th ♭5 chord.

The type of chord that can be built by taking alternate notes from each degree of a natural minor scale is always the same for each particular scale degree, regardless of the key.

All minor keys based on the natural minor scale have the following pattern of chords:

I	II	III	IV	V	VI	VII
minor 7th	minor 7th ♭5	major 7th	minor 7th	minor 7th	major 7th	dominant 7th

Below are these chords built from the A, E, B, F#, D, G and C natural minor scales.

Degree:	I	II	III	IV	V	VI	VII
A minor:	Am7	Bm7♭5	Cmaj7	Dm7	Em7	Fmaj7	G7
E minor:	Em7	F#m7♭5	Gmaj7	Am7	Bm7	Cmaj7	D7
B minor:	Bm7	C#m7♭5	Dmaj7	Em7	F#m7	Gmaj7	A7
F# minor:	F#m7	G#m7♭5	Amaj7	Bm7	C#m7	Dmaj7	E7
D minor:	Dm7	Em7♭5	Fmaj7	Gm7	Am7	B♭maj7	C7
G minor:	Gm7	Am7♭5	B♭maj7	Cm7	Dm7	E♭maj7	F7
C minor:	Cm7	Dm7♭5	E♭maj7	Fm7	Gm7	A♭maj7	B♭7

Notice that the chords built on the 1st, 4th and 5th degrees are minor 7th chords, the chords built on the 3rd and 6th degrees are major 7th chords, the chord built on the 7th degree is a dominant 7th chord and the chord built on the 2nd degree is a minor 7th ♭5 chord.

Degrees of the scale and the chords that are built on them, are traditionally, and still widely, identified using Roman numerals. This system provides a useful shortcut for writing chords, as it identifies the 'type' of chord as well as the 'position' of the chord in the scale. Below are the various seventh chords that are built from the C major and A natural minor scales identified using the Roman numeral system. By using the formulae below you can work out which seventh chords can be built from any major or natural minor scale.

C major	Triad:	Cmaj7	Dm7	Em7	Fmaj7	G7	Am7	Bm7♭5
	Roman numerals:	Imaj7	IIm7	IIIm7	IVmaj7	V7	VIm7	VIIm7♭5

A natural minor	Triad:	Am7	Bm7♭5	Cmaj7	Dm7	Em7	Fmaj7	G7
	Roman numerals:	Im7	IIm7♭5	♭IIImaj7	IVm7	Vm7	♭VImaj7	♭VII7

Below you will find a brief explanation as to why the chords from the natural minor scale are numbered in this way when using the Roman numeral system. In the exam, however, you will only be asked to identify, or write out the pattern of chords.

Supplementary explanation

The chords built from the natural minor scale are numbered in comparison to the chords built from the major scale with the same keynote. The flat sign before the chords built on the 3rd, 6th and 7th degrees indicates that the roots of these chords are one half step (semitone) lower than the roots of the corresponding chords built from the major scale with the same keynote.

For example, in the key of C major the 3rd, 6th and 7th notes are E, A and B. In the scale of C natural minor the 3rd, 6th and 7th notes are E♭, A♭ and B♭. Therefore the roots of the chords built on these degrees of the C natural minor scale are all a half step lower than the roots of the chords built on same degrees of the C major scale.

Nashville numbering

Some musicians (particularly in the USA) prefer to use standard numbers in place of Roman numerals – this method of identifying chords is called the 'Nashville Numbering System'. An outline of this system of chord identification has been provided in the Grade Three book. In the exam, answers can be expressed using either system, providing you are consistent in your usage.

Technical names

Chords that occur on each degree of the scale have names that originate in classical music terminology. In popular music, only the three main chords of each key are still referred to by these names on occasion:

- The chord that occurs on the first degree of the scale is known as the *tonic*.

- The chord that occurs on the fourth degree of the scale is known as the *subdominant*.

- The chord that occurs on the fifth degree of the scale is known as the *dominant*.

cadences

Cadences are musical 'punctuation marks' created by using a combination of chords that imply a resting place. A minimum of two chords have to be used in order to create the *resolution*. Cadences nearly always appear at the end of songs, however they also occur in other places during the course of a song, such as at the end of a phrase or verse.

Historically, two cadences that have been used extensively both in classical and popular music are the *V – I cadence* (also called the *perfect cadence*) and the *IV – I cadence* (also called the *plagal cadence*).

The *V – I cadence* is the cadence which creates the strongest and most complete ending to a phrase. In the key of C major this can be played as either G to C, or G7 to C. By playing the V chord as a dominant 7th chord (rather than just a major triad) a

stronger sounding cadence is created. Consequently, V – I cadences are often played as V7 – I.

The *IV – I cadence* is another cadence which is often used to end a musical phrase, although it is more subtle than the V – I cadence. In major keys the IV chord can be played either as a major triad or as a major seventh chord. So the IV – I cadence in C major can be played as F to C or Fmaj7 to C.

In both cadences the I chord may also be played as a major seventh chord.

V – I cadences and IV – I cadences are also used in music based on natural minor scales. As with major keys, the V – I cadence is the stronger and more final sounding cadence, whilst the IV – I cadence is more subtle. In both cases either minor triads or minor 7th chords can be used. The two cadences in A natural minor can therefore be played in any of the following ways:

V – I cadence: Em to Am, Em7 to Am, Em to Am7 or Em7 to Am7

IV – I cadence: Dm to Am, Dm7 to Am, Dm to Am7 or Dm7 to Am7

constructing chord progressions

There are many different approaches to writing chord progressions, but deciding how effective the chords will sound in any particular combination is the most important consideration. Here are a few tips on writing chord progressions that may be helpful:

- So that you can choose from the full range of chords, you need to know all the common chords that are in the key. You can work them out by using the formulae given previously.

- Starting the chord progression with the *tonic chord* will help to instantly define the pitch and tonality of the key.

- Using a V – I, or IV – I, cadence at the end of the progression will help to create a sense of 'reaching a resting point' or a feeling of 'arriving home'.

For example, this progression in the key of A major starts with the tonic chord and ends with a V – I cadence.

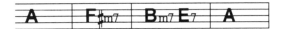

This progression in the key of C minor starts with the tonic chord and ends with a IV – I cadence.

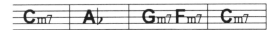

Although both these progressions use cadences to indicate the end of a musical phrase, it is not essential that phrases end in this way. When writing chord progressions, the most important consideration is *do the chords you have used create the musical effect you intended?*

improvisation

Major and pentatonic major scales are used for improvising in major keys. For example, if a chord progression uses chords built from the A major scale, then either the A major or A pentatonic major scale would be an appropriate scale to use for improvising.

Natural minor and pentatonic minor scales are used for improvising in minor keys. For example, if a chord progression uses chords built from the F# natural minor scale, then either the F# natural minor or F# pentatonic minor scale would be an appropriate scale to use for improvising.

Identifying which key the chords in a progression belong to will help you decide which scale to use for improvisation. Because the chords from any major scale and its relative natural minor are the same, it is important to look at how the chord progression is structured in order to correctly identify the key. Normally, a chord progression will start and finish on the I (tonic) chord, and this will indicate whether the progression is in the major or relative minor key.

For example, in the following chord progressions all the chords occur in both the keys of A major and F# minor, but the first progression is in the key of A major whilst the second is in the key of F# minor (the relative minor of A major).

A maj7	F#m7	D maj7	E7	A maj7
Imaj7	VIm7	IVmaj7	V7	Imaj7

The A major scale, or the A pentatonic major scale, would be a good scale choice for improvisation over the progression shown above.

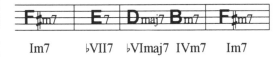

F#m7	E7	D maj7	Bm7	F#m7
Im7	♭VII7	♭VImaj7	IVm7	Im7

The F# natural minor scale, or the F# pentatonic minor scale, would be a good scale choice for improvisation.

When you are writing a chord progression to be used as a backing for improvisation the same process as described above applies. Firstly, work out the possible chords that can built from each degree of that scale, and then experiment with different possible combinations until you come up with a progression that you like. Remember that using a V-I or IV-I cadence is a straightforward and effective way to create an ending to a progression.

the exam

Below are some examples of the types of questions that candidates may be asked in this section of the exam. If you can't answer a question then carefully re-read the preceding chapter and, if necessary, refer to the preceding books in this series.

Q1 Using chord symbols, write out the various 7th chords that are built from each degree of the B♭ major scale.

A1. _____

Q2. Using chord symbols, write out the various 7th chords that are built from each degree of the F# natural minor scale.

A2. _____

Q3. What type of cadence is formed between the last chord in bar 3 and the chord in bar 4?

| A | F#m7 | E7 Dmaj7 | A |

A3. _____

Q4. Using at least three different chords, write a four bar chord progression in the key of E♭ major with the last two bars forming a IV-I (plagal) cadence.

A4.

Q5. Name a scale that could be used effectively for improvising over the following chord progression.

| Bm7 | Gmaj7 | F#m7 | Em7 Bm |

A5. _____

Q6. Using at least three different chords, write a four bar chord progression over which the scale of A pentatonic major could be used for improvising.

A6.

Section Six – transposition

In this section of the exam you will be asked to demonstrate your skills in transposing chord progressions. In particular you will be asked to transpose a chord progression either up or down a whole step (whole tone) or a half step (semitone) within a range of keys up to three sharps or three flats.

the theory

There are two different methods that you can use to transpose chord progressions. Both methods will give exactly the same result.

chord numbers

Identify the key of the original chord progression and work out the chord numbers for each of the chords. Using the chord numbers then work out the chords in the new key.

For example, to transpose the following chord progression into the key of B♭ major, the first step is to identify the key of the progression.

| A | B♭m7 | E7 | A |

The above chord progression is in the key of A major because: the progression starts and ends on an A major triad; all the chords are in the key of A major and the movement from E7 to A forms a V-I (perfect) cadence in the key of A major.

Having worked out the key of the progression next identify the tonic chord, which would have the chord number I. From this, the other chord numbers can then be worked out. You can check that you have worked them out correctly by ensuring that the chord type for each degree corresponds to the standard major scale pattern of triads and seventh chords.

The chord numbers for the above progression are:

I	IIm7	V7	I
A	B♭m7	E7	A

To transpose the chord progression to B♭ major, you need to work out what the I, IIm,

and V7 chords are, in the key of B♭ major. To do this, count up the degrees of the B♭ major scale to find the root of each chord (the 2nd of B♭ is C, the 5th of B♭ is F). Remember, the chord quality for each chord remains the same as in the original key, therefore the chord progression transposed into the key of B♭ major will be:

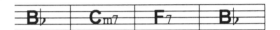

| B♭ | Cm7 | F7 | B♭ |

intervals

Another way to transpose the chord progression is to change the root note of each chord by the interval requested. For the Grade Four exam, this will be either up or down a whole step (whole tone) or half step (semitone). You work this out, by first identifying the original key, as above, and then by deciding if the key you have to transpose the progression into is a whole step, or half step, above or below the original key. In this instance, B♭ is one half step above A: so for this transposition the root note of each chord needs to be moved up one half step. As in the previous method, the chord types stay the same as in the original key.

- The A major chord would move up a half step to become B♭ major.
- The Bm7 chord would move up a half step to become Cm7.
- The E7 chord would move up a half step to become F7.

With both these methods it is essential that you take account of any sharps or flats that occur in the new key so that the correct enharmonic spelling is used.

the exam

Below are some examples of the types of questions that candidates may be asked in this section of the exam. If you can't answer a question, then carefully re-read the preceding chapter. Once you've worked through these questions you can check your answers by looking in the back of the book.

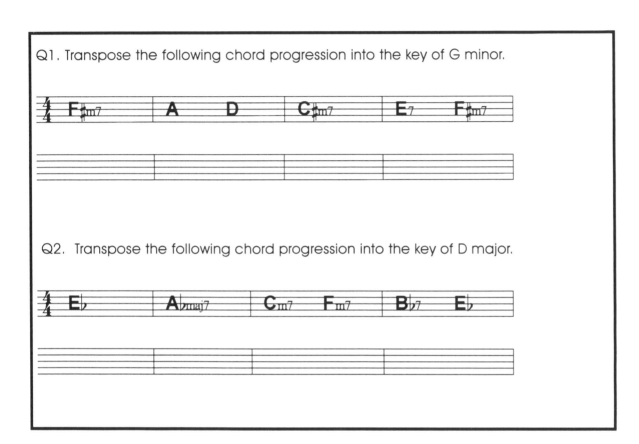

Q1. Transpose the following chord progression into the key of G minor.

Q2. Transpose the following chord progression into the key of D major.

Section Seven – sample answers

Note that all the answers below are 'sample answers' and for several questions there are a range of other answers that would also be acceptable.

Section One – scales and keys   [Max. 20 marks]

A1.   F# G# A B C# D E# F#

A2.   C E♭ F G B♭ C

A3.   1 2 ♭3 4 5 ♭6 7 8

A4.

or

A5.

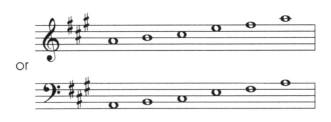

or

Section Two – chords   [Max. 20 marks]

A1.   A E A

A2.   Dsus4

A3.   1 ♭3 ♭5 ♭7

A4.   sus4, 5th 'power chord'. (sus2 is also correct)

A5.   Flattened seventh (or minor seventh)

A6.

Section Three – rhythm notation *[Max. 10 marks]*

A1.

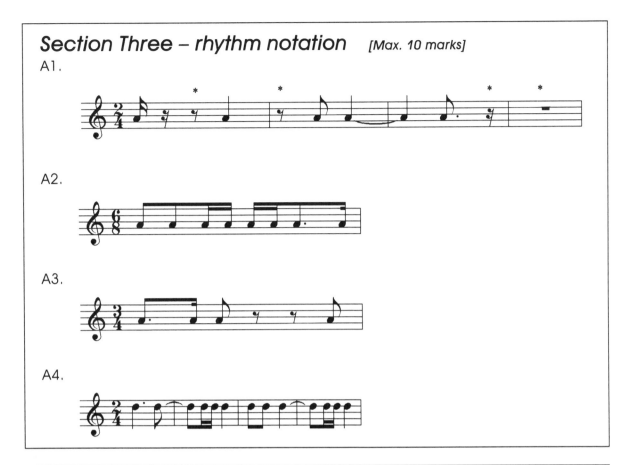

A2.

A3.

A4.

Section Four – knowledge of popular music *[Max. 15 marks]*

A1. Johnny Rotten – vocalist, Steve Jones – guitarist, Paul Cook – drummer, (Glen Matlock or Sid Vicious – bassist would also be acceptable)

A2. The I-Threes. They added a gospel/soul sound to the music.

A3. The Piper At The Gates Of Dawn – 1960s, Dark Side of the Moon – 1970s.

A4. Distortion and wah-wah.

A5. To play melodies or riffs as part of a horn section, or to play melodies or improvise as a soloist.

A6. Gradually increasing in volume from playing very softly to playing moderately strongly.

A7.

Section Five – harmony   [Max. 25 marks]

A1.   B♭maj7 Cm7 Dm7 E♭maj7 F7 Gm7 Am7♭5

A2.   F#m7 G#m7♭5 Amaj7 Bm7 C#m7 Dmaj7 E7

A3.   IV – I (Plagal cadence would also be correct).

A4.

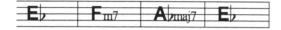

A5.   B natural minor (or B pentatonic minor)

A6.

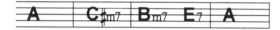

Section Six – transposition   [Max. 10 marks]

A1.

A2.

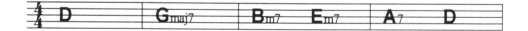

Examination Entry Form for LCM
Popular Music Theory examination.

GRADE FOUR

PLEASE COMPLETE CLEARLY USING BLOCK CAPITAL LETTERS

SESSION (Summer/Winter): _____   YEAR: _____

Preferred Examination Centre (if known): _____
If left blank, you will be examined at the nearest examination centre to your home address.

Candidate Details:

Candidate Name (as to appear on certificate):

_____

Address: _____

_____

_____   Postcode: _____

Tel. No. (day): _____   (evening): _____

Teacher Details:

Teacher Name (as to appear on certificate): _____

Registry Tutor Code (if applicable): _____

Address: _____

_____   Postcode: _____

Tel. No. (day): _____   (evening): _____

The standard LCM entry form is NOT valid for Popular Music Theory entries. Entry to the examination is only possible via this original form.

Photocopies of this form will not be accepted under *any* circumstances.

IMPORTANT NOTES

- It is the candidate's responsibility to have knowledge of, and comply with, the current syllabus requirements. Where candidates are entered for examinations by teachers, the teacher must take responsibility that candidates are entered in accordance with the current syllabus requirements. In particular, from 2005 it is important to check that the contents of this book match the syllabus that is valid at the time of entry.

- For candidates with special needs, a letter giving details should be attached.

- Theory dates are the same worldwide and are fixed annually by LCM. Details of entry deadlines and examination dates are obtainable from the Examinations Registry.

- Submission of this entry is an undertaking to abide by the current regulations as listed in the current syllabus and any subsequent regulations updates published by the LCM / Examinations Registry.

- UK entries should be sent to The Examinations Registry, Registry House, Churchill Mews, Dennett Rd, Croydon, Surrey CR0 3JH

- Overseas entrants should contact the LCM / Examinations Registry for details of their international representatives.

Examination Fee   £ _____

Late Entry Fee (if applicable)   £ _____

Total amount submitted: £ _____

Cheques or postal orders should be made payable to The Examinations Registry.
Entries cannot be made by credit card.

A current list of fees is available from the Examinations Registry.

The Examinations Registry
Registry House
Churchill Mews
Dennett Road
Croydon
Surrey, U.K.
CR0 3JH

Tel: 020 8665 7666
Fax: 020 8665 7667
Email: ExamRegistry@aol.com